Grow a Pizza Garden

By
John Benzee

Welcome to the garden! Here you'll learn to grow some ingredients that make up a tasty pizza. The best pizza uses the freshest toppings, so let's get growing.

Growing List

Tomato

Basil

Oregano

Extra toppings

Growing Plan

Grab these supplies and plan out your garden. Make sure you have everything to begin. Don't forget me, seeds!

Find a space to grow, either in the ground or in some pots. Good, healthy soil is important too. Add some compost or fertilizer to give plants a boost.

Weather and water: Plants need a sunny spot and should be grown in the spring and summer. Don't forget to water them!

Tools: They help get the job done.

Grow Tomatoes

Let's grow tomatoes. Choose a paste or plum variety for pizza sauce, such as San Marzano, Roma, Amish Paste, or Margherita.

Step 1

Tomatoes are best grown by first starting them inside. After they are big and strong enough, they will be transplanted outside.

Fill some small pots with potting soil. Tap down lightly on top, smoothing the soil so you have an even planting surface.

Step 2

Place a few seeds in each pot, following the instructions on the seed packet. They should only be about 1/8 to 1/4 of an inch deep (3-6mm). Then cover the seeds with a little bit of soil.

Make sure to label each pot so you know what variety you planted. Popsicle sticks, cut-up milk jugs, or even clothespins make great plant labels.

Step 3 Find a warm and sunny spot, like a windowsill, to put your pots. Make sure the soil stays moist. In 7 to 14 days the seeds should sprout, and the seedlings should appear out of the soil.

Once the seeds sprout, rotate the pots every few days so the seedlings don't stretch and grow spindly. If they get leggy (tall and thin), they need more light.

Step 4

Once your tomato seedlings are big enough, bring them outside for a few hours each day to get used to the outdoor weather. This process is called hardening off and helps the tomato seedlings be strong enough to endure the wind, rain, and weather.

Step 5

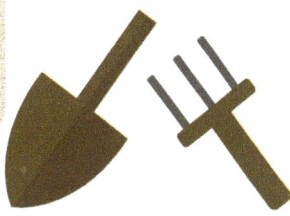

Time to transplant the tomatoes into their permanent home. Make sure the weather is consistently warm. Prepare the soil, either in a large pot or in a garden. Remember, find a sunny spot.

Make a hole at least 8 inches (16 cm) deep in the soil. Carefully pull the seedlings out of their pots, holding onto the stem at the base of the plant. Gently place a plant in each hole and cover the roots up. Don't forget to give your plants a drink.

Make sure to keep your labels!

Step 6

Take care of your tomato plants. Help them grow big and strong by giving them water, fertilizer, and support. Stake or cage tomatoes so they grow tall and upright.

Step 7

Watch your tomatoes grow. When the green tomatoes ripen to red, they are ready to be picked. Gather a bunch so you can make tomato sauce.

Save some of your seeds! Take a few big, healthy tomatoes, slice them open, and squeeze out the seeds. Dry the seeds and store them to plant next year.

Grow Basil

Let's grow basil. Any variety will do, but popular types are Sweet, Genovese, or Mammoth.

Step 1

Basil can be grown by first starting it inside, then moving it outside, or by directly seeding outside when it is warm enough.

Fill some small pots with potting soil. Tap down lightly on top, smoothing the soil so you have a flat planting surface.

Step 2

Basil seeds can be lightly spread on the surface of the soil, then lightly covered up. There is no need to make a hole. Don't forget to label your pots.

Lightly mist the soil when finished. Make sure the soil stays moist.

Step 3 Find a warm and sunny spot to put your pots. Make sure the soil stays moist. In 5 to 10 days the seeds should sprout.

Step 4 Once the basil plants are big enough, move them outside. If there are too many seedlings in a pot, thin them by cutting a few down to make room for others. If a plant gets too big, move it to a bigger pot or plant it in the ground.

Step 5

Care for your basil plants as they continue to grow. Pinch back the leaves if a plant is getting too tall. This will encourage it to grow bushy. If a plant starts to flower, the flowers can be cut off so the plant grows more leaves.

Harvest basil regularly by gently picking off some of its leaves. Even if you don't need it, continue to harvest so that the plant will continue to produce more leaves. Remember to give them a drink.

Grow Oregano

Growing oregano is very similar to growing basil. Pick a tasty variety, such as Common, Greek, or Italian. Oregano has a stronger and earthier taste than basil.

Step 1

Follow the steps for growing basil. Fill a few pots with soil, sow your seeds, and put the pots in a warm, sunny place.

Step 2

In 7 to 14 days the seeds should sprout. Make sure the seedlings have enough water, but not too much.

Step 3

Thin seedlings so that the biggest and healthiest plants remain. You can then transplant them into a larger pot or into the ground.

Step 4

Continue to care for your oregano plants. To harvest leaves, pinch or cut a few sprigs (bunches of leaves) off.

Oregano can be eaten fresh or dried to be used later. To dry oregano, gather a few handfuls of leaves. Lay them flat on a paper towel, tray, or screen inside. Keep the leaves away from moisture and wind.

Another method is to tie sprigs of oregano together and hang them to dry. Both drying methods can take up to two weeks and then the dried leaves should be put into containers. These drying methods work for basil too.

Grow Onions

Step 1

Onions are a tasty topping that often is added to a pizza. Growing onions is fairly easy. Choose a purple/ red variety, such as Ruby, Wethersfield, or Southport.

Onions can be started as seeds, but it will take almost 100 days for them to mature. That is a long time to wait for pizza!

Instead, choose onion sets or transplants, which are small bulbs that already have a head start. These will mature in 30 to 50 days.

Step 2

Prepare your planting area, either a large pot, long garden row, or raised bed. Dig a shallow furrow and put the onion sets or transplants 1 inch (3 cm) deep and 3-4 inches (8-10 cm) apart. The tips should be pointing up. Cover lightly with soil.

Step 3 Care for your onions as they continue to grow. Apply fertilizer or compost every three weeks. This will help grow big bulbs. Water when necessary. When the bulbs begin to appear above the soil, stop fertilizing. Your onions are almost ready.

Step 4 Onions are ready to harvest when the stalks are yellowing, dry, and falling over. Grasp the stalk near the bulb and pull up. Carefully handle the bulbs to prevent damage. Cut off the roots and the stalk.

Step 5 If you are not planning on eating the onions right away, they will need to be dried or cured. Put the onions in a place with well-circulating air for two weeks until the outer scales are dry. Then store them in a cool place until needed. They will store best at 40 to 60°F (4 to 15°C).

Grow Peppers

Let's grow peppers for a flavorful topping to pizza. Choose a sweet variety, such as Bell or Sweet Banana. Growing peppers is a lot like tomatoes, so review growing tomatoes if you need to.

Step 1

After preparing the soil for planting indoors, sow the seeds into the soil about 1/4 inch (6mm) deep, about 8 weeks before you want to plant outside. Lightly cover and keep them moist.

Step 2

Make sure the seeds get enough warmth so they can sprout. Once the seeds have sprouted, continue to make sure they get enough sunlight. When they are big enough, harden off the plants before planting them in a large pot or into the ground. Provide support too.

Step 3 Take care of your pepper plants. Water regularly and make sure to remove any weeds that may pop up around your plants. Soon your plants should flower.

Step 4 A few weeks after flowering and setting fruit, your peppers may be ready for harvest. If the peppers are big enough, they can be picked green, or you can wait until they turn yellow or red. If you keep picking peppers the plant will produce more.

Pizza Time

Now that you've grown most of the ingredients to make a pizza, it's time to make one. You can rely on local farmers or grocers to make the dough and cheese, but you can do the rest.

Ingredients from your garden

Tomatoes
About 15-20

Basil
1-2 handfuls

Oregano
1 handful

Pepper
One

Onion
One

Other ingredients and supplies

Olive oil
2 tablespoons

Garlic
1 clove

Sugar
1 teaspoon

Salt
1/2 teaspoon

Medium pot **Hand blender** **Knife and spoon**

Mozzarella Cheese
4 ounces (150g)

Baking sheet and cutting board

Plan ahead and prepare your space before continuing.

Pizza dough or shell

Ask an adult to help you cook. Be safe.

Recipe for Pizza Sauce

The following recipe will make enough sauce for about 4 pizzas. It will take about 40-60 minutes.

Step 1

Remove any tomato stems and rinse the tomatoes with water. Cut them in half.

Step 2

With a spoon or knife, remove the seeds and inside parts of the tomatoes. Set the tomatoes aside for later.

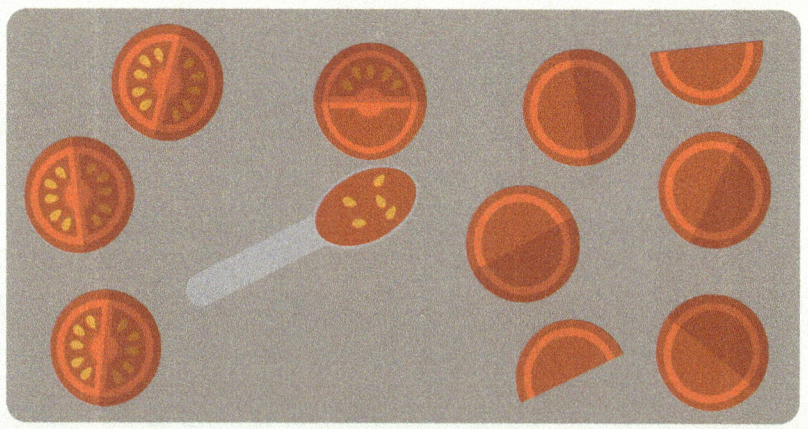

Step 3

Pour the olive oil into a medium pot. Heat to medium-low.

Step 4

Carefully chop the garlic into small pieces, then add to the oil. Cook for 2-3 minutes, then reduce heat.

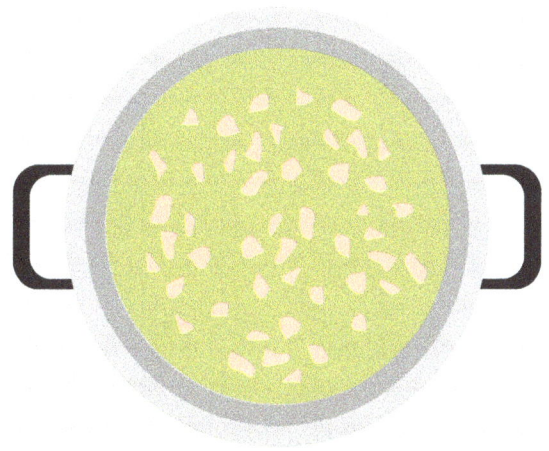

Step 5

Add the tomatoes to the pot.

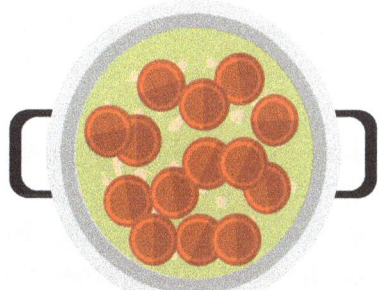

Step 6 Take a few basil or oregano leaves (your choice), chop them up, and add them to the tomatoes.

Step 7 Stir in the salt and the sugar, which will reduce the acidity of the tomatoes.

Step 8

Cover the pot with a lid and let the mixture simmer on low heat for 30 minutes. Stir occasionally.

Step 9

Take a hand mixer (or food mill or processor) and grind the tomatoes into the sauce. This should break up the tomato skins.

Step 10

The sauce is almost complete. Continue to simmer if you want the sauce to be thicker. Otherwise, turn off the heat and add more basil or oregano leaves, if desired.

Step 11

You can now use the pizza sauce for your pizza. Store extra sauce in a container in the fridge for 2-3 days.

Recipe for Pizza

The following recipe makes 1 pizza. It will take about 15 minutes.

Step 1 — Preheat the oven to 430°F (220°C).

Step 2 — Roll out the dough into a circle or use a premade pizza shell. Put it on a baking sheet.

Step 3 — Spread your pizza sauce over the dough, leaving a small border on the edge.

Step 4 Top with mozzarella cheese, either as slices or as shredded cheese.

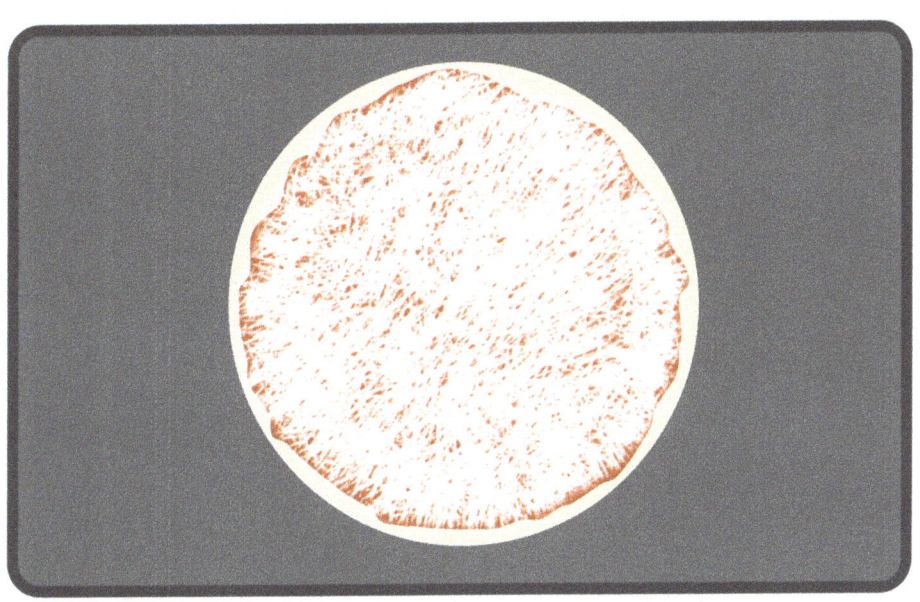

Step 5 If you would like to add other toppings, such as peppers or onions, cut them into slices and add a few pieces to your pizza.

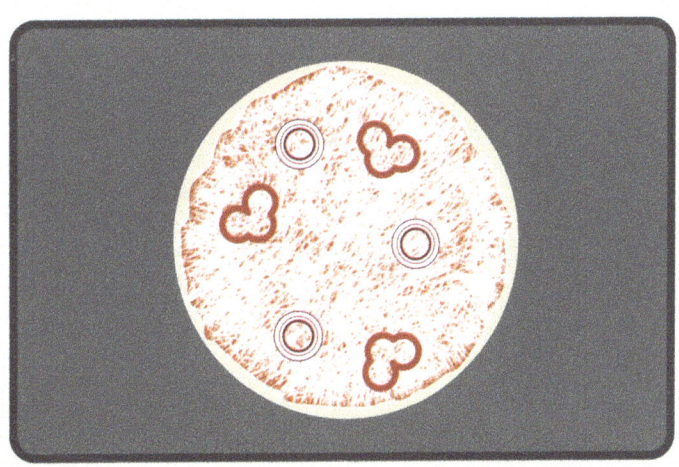

Step 6

Place the pizza in the oven and bake until the cheese is melted and the crust is golden brown, about 8 to 10 minutes.

Step 7

Once the pizza is cooked, remove it from the oven. Take a few basil leaves, tear them into a few pieces and scatter them over the pizza.

Step 8   Time to eat! Enjoy your homegrown pizza.

29

Other varieties of pizza

There are other recipes for making pizza, depending on what you want to put on it.

Instead of using tomato sauce, slice a few tomatoes and add them to the pizza.

Try some fun toppings, such as pineapple, olives, mushrooms, or spinach.

You can even get creative and make watermelon into a pizza. Slice up a watermelon, add cheese, basil or mint, and enjoy.

Happy gardening and cooking!

Grow a Pizza Garden
Copyright © 2022 by John Benzee
All illustrations and text by John Benzee

All rights reserved.
No part of this book may be used or reproduced in any manner whatsoever without permission, except in the case of brief quotations in critical articles or reviews.

Published by Split Seed Press; Clarence, NY
ISBN: 978-0-9997379-5-8 (hardcover)
ISBN: 978-0-9997379-6-5 (paperback)
ISBN: 978-1-7333197-1-3 (eBook)

First edition
Library of Congress Control Number: 2022905771

Visit johnbenzee.com for more information
Typeset in Nunito; Illustrations created in Affinity Designer.

Dedication: To all gardeners and pizza lovers everywhere.

Publisher's Cataloging-In-Publication Data:
Names: Benzee, John, 1995— author, illustrator.
Title: Grow a pizza garden / by John Benzee.
Description: Clarence : Split Seed Press, 2022. | Series: Grow and Eat Series. |
Summary: A step-by-step gardening guide and cookbook for kids to grow the ingredients to make a fresh, homemade pizza.
Identifiers: LCCN: 2022905771 | ISBN 9780999737958 (hardcover) | ISBN 9780999737965 (paperback) | ISBN 9781733319713 (ebook)
Subjects: LCSH: Vegetable Gardening—Juvenile literature. | Herb gardening--Juvenile literature. | Cooking—Juvenile literature. | BISAC: JUVENILE NONFICTION / Gardening.
Classification: SB 457.B46 2022 | DDC 635--dc23

10 9 8 7 6 5 4 3 2 1

www.ingramcontent.com/pod-product-compliance
Lightning Source LLC
Chambersburg PA
CBHW061149010526
44118CB00026B/2918